Yum! Yuck!

A Fol...ounds

LINDA SUE PARK
JULIA DURANGO

Illustrated by
SUE RAMÁ

Charlesbridge

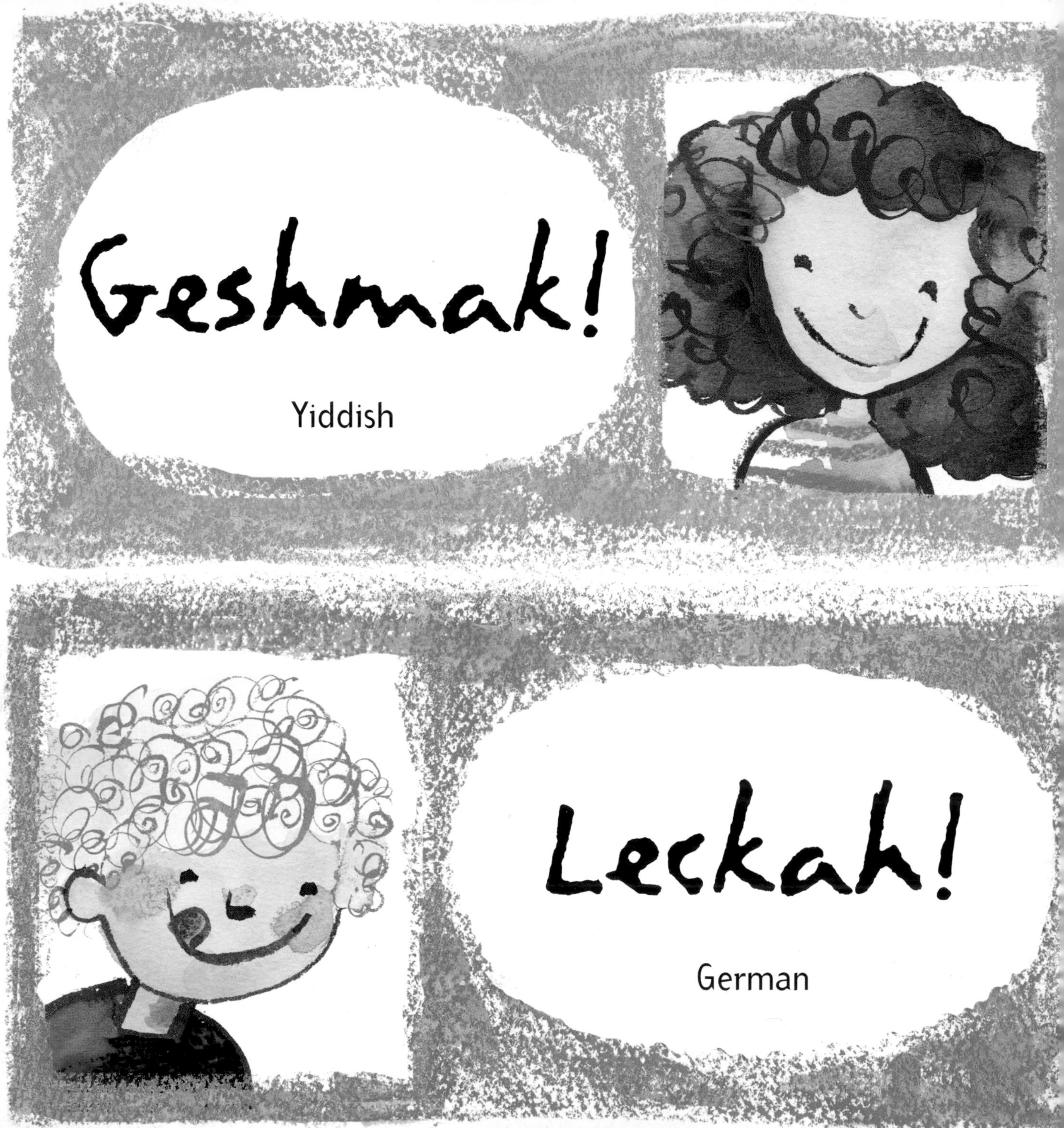
Geshmak!
Yiddish
Leckah!
German

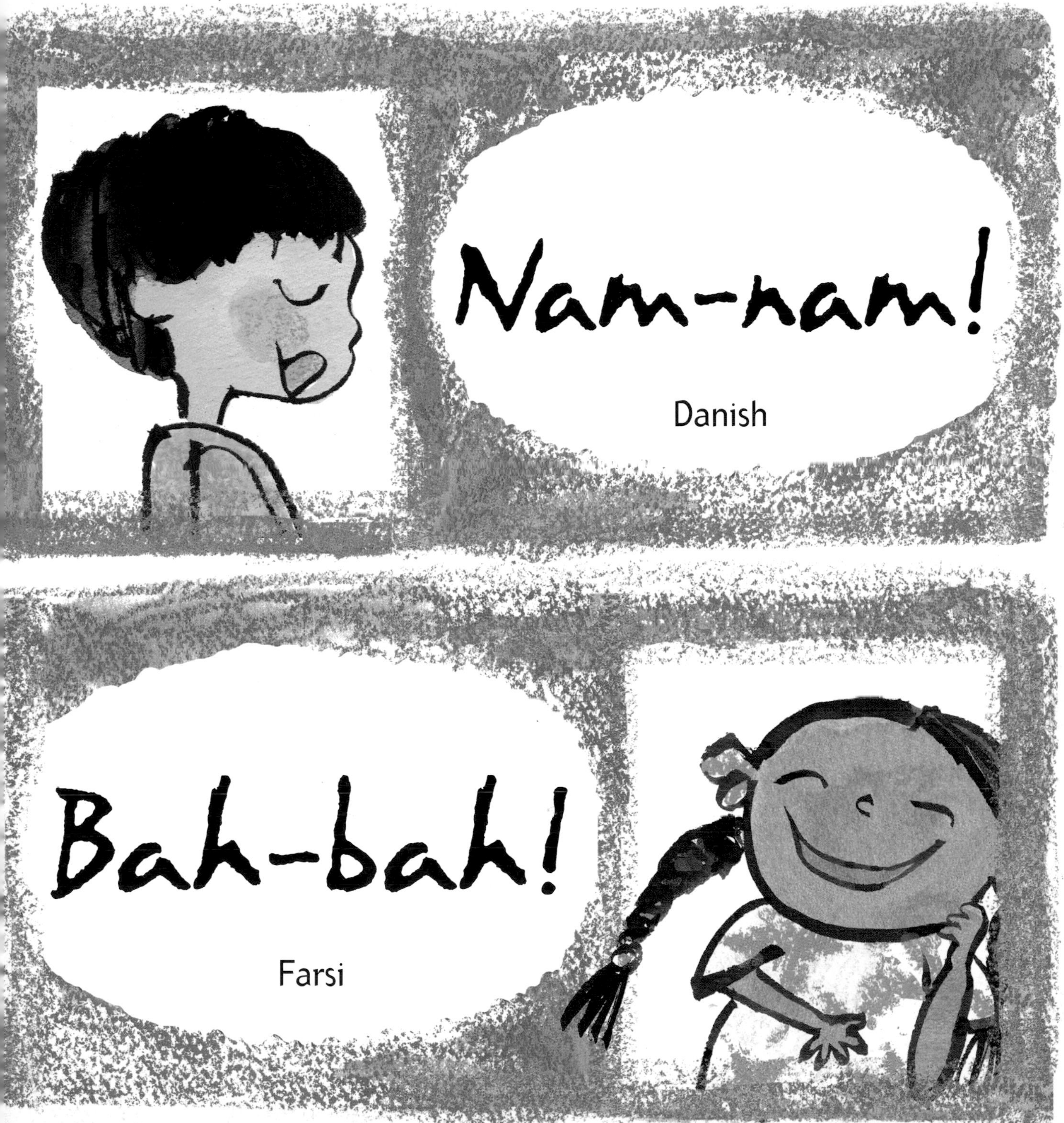
Nam-nam!
Danish
Bah-bah!
Farsi

Yum!

English

Ha-ha!

English

Oy!

Polish

Oo-wah!

Japanese

Ah-choo!

English

¡Guácala!

Spanish

Pwah!

French

Foo!

Russian

Oo-wek!

Korean

Yuck!

English

Voy!

Farsi

Vov-vov!

Swedish

Po-po!

Greek

Hui!

German

Evviva!

Italian

Hwan-ho!

Vietnamese

Spices

Hurray!

English

¡Yupi!

Evviva!

AUTHORS' NOTE:

Translating "people sounds" isn't always easy. First we collected sounds as they are usually heard or written in their original languages. Then we rewrote many of those sounds so that an English speaker would know how to pronounce them. For example, we changed the spelling of the Polish word **oj** to **oy**. This is called phonetic translation. But sometimes language pronunciation can vary by country, by region, or even by generation. Do you say **to-MAY-toes** or **to-MAH-toes**? While both pronunciations are correct, you're more likely to say **to-MAY-toes** if you live in North America and **to-MAH-toes** if you live in England. Differences in pronunciation happen in other languages, too.

Hwan-ho!

Ballay-ballay!

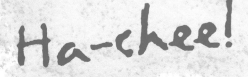

Et-chee! Ah-bushku!

Likewise, while each non-English sound in this book is one way to translate the corresponding English sound, it is certainly not the only way. For instance, a native speaker from Colombia might say **yupi**, while children from other Spanish-speaking countries might say **hurra**, **viva**, **bravo**, or **olé** instead. This occurs in English, too. A North American might say **yikes**, whereas someone from England might say **blimey**. The languages we speak change and grow, just like we do!

Language Notes:

Farsi: An official language in Iran, Tajikistan, and Afghanistan.
Tamil: An official language in India, Sri Lanka, and Singapore.
Yoruba: A language that originated in Nigeria.
Punjabi: The official language of the Punjab state in India.

Ha-chee! Ap-soo!

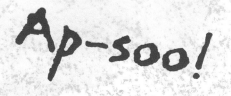

Published by Charlesbridge
85 Main Street
Watertown, MA 02472
(617) 926-0329
www.charlesbridge.com

Library of Congress Cataloging-in-Publication Data
Park, Linda Sue.
   Yum! Yuck! : a foldout book of people sounds / Linda Sue Park, Julia Durango ; illustrated by Sue Ramá.
      p. cm.
   ISBN 1-57091-659-4 (hardcover)
1. Grammar, Comparative and general—Interjections—Juvenile literature. 2. Grammar, Comparative and general—Exclamations—Juvenile literature. I. Durango, Julia. II. Ramá, Sue. III. Title.
P287.P37   2005
418—dc22   2004018955

Printed in China
(hc) 10 9 8 7 6 5 4 3 2 1

Illustrations done in ink line, water-soluble crayon, and watercolor, then combined and
   manipulated digitally
Display type and text type set in Lettres Eclatees and Arbitrary
Color separated, printed, and bound by Jade Productions
Production supervision by Brian G. Walker
Designed by Sue Ramá